Working Animals
Search-and-Rescue Animals

by Julie Murray

Dash!
LEVELED READERS
An Imprint of Abdo Zoom • abdobooks.com

2

Dash!
LEVELED READERS

2

Level 1 – Beginning
Short and simple sentences with familiar words or patterns for children who are beginning to understand how letters and sounds go together.

Level 2 – Emerging
Longer words and sentences with more complex language patterns for readers who are practicing common words and letter sounds.

Level 3 – Transitional
More developed language and vocabulary for readers who are becoming more independent.

THIS BOOK CONTAINS RECYCLED MATERIALS

abdobooks.com

Published by Abdo Zoom, a division of ABDO, PO Box 398166, Minneapolis, Minnesota 55439. Copyright © 2020 by Abdo Consulting Group, Inc. International copyrights reserved in all countries. No part of this book may be reproduced in any form without written permission from the publisher. Dash!™ is a trademark and logo of Abdo Zoom.

Printed in the United States of America, North Mankato, Minnesota.
052019
092019

Photo Credits: Alamy, iStock, Shutterstock
Production Contributors: Kenny Abdo, Jennie Forsberg, Grace Hansen, John Hansen
Design Contributors: Dorothy Toth, Neil Klinepier

Library of Congress Control Number: 2018963314

Publisher's Cataloging in Publication Data

Names: Murray, Julie, author.
Title: Search-and-rescue animals / by Julie Murray.
Description: Minneapolis, Minnesota : Abdo Zoom, 2020 | Series: Working animals | Includes online resources and index.
Identifiers: ISBN 9781532127335 (lib. bdg.) | ISBN 9781532128318 (ebook) | ISBN 9781532128806 (Read-to-me ebook)
Subjects: LCSH: Working animals--Juvenile literature. | Search dogs--Juvenile literature. | Rescue dogs--Juvenile literature.
Classification: DDC 636.7--dc23

Table of Contents

Search-and-Rescue Animals . . 4

Types of Rescue Dogs 12

More Facts 22

Glossary 23

Index 24

Online Resources 24

Search-and-Rescue Animals

Search-and-rescue animals do important work. They look for people who are lost, trapped, or missing.

These animals need special training. They work with their **handlers** as part of a team.

Dogs are the most common animals used. Horses can be used too.

Some animals work after a **natural disaster**. Ace looks for people after an earthquake.

Types of Rescue Dogs

Many dogs are trained for a certain situation. Air-scent dogs pick up smells in the air.

Trailing dogs sniff an item belonging to the lost person. Then they sniff the ground to pick up the person's scent.

Snow search dogs find people buried in the snow. They can find a person under 15 feet of snow!

Water rescue dogs save drowning **victims**. They help get them to a safe place.

These animals work hard! They save thousands of lives each year.

More Facts

- St. Bernards were the first search-and-rescue dogs. They were used around 1665 in the Swiss Alps.

- Cadaver dogs are used to find dead bodies. They pick up the body's scent.

- About 350 search-and-rescue dogs worked at the 9/11 site after the deadly attack.

Glossary

handler – a person who trains and has charge of an animal.

natural disaster – a natural event such as a flood, earthquake, or hurricane that causes great damage.

victim – someone who is hurt, injured, or killed by a person, group, or event.

Index

air-scent dog 13

dogs 8, 10, 13, 14, 16, 18

earthquake 10

handler 6

horses 8

snow search dogs 16

trailing dog 14

training 6

uses 5, 13, 14, 18

water rescue dogs 18

Online Resources

Booklinks
NONFICTION NETWORK
FREE! ONLINE NONFICTION RESOURCES

To learn more about search-and-rescue animals, please visit **abdobooklinks.com** or scan this QR code. These links are routinely monitored and updated to provide the most current information available.